THE AMERICAN HOUSE STYLES OF ARCHITECTURE
Coloring Book

A. G. SMITH

Dover Publications, Inc.
New York

PUBLISHER'S NOTE

The domestic architecture of the United States is rich and varied, boasting the homes of the first Americans—the Indians—as well as the many European styles that have flourished on these shores. All, however, have been subject to adaptation and modification to make them responsive to changing needs. This variety has nurtured architects whose influence has been profound—H. H. Richardson, Louis Sullivan and Frank Lloyd Wright among them.

In this work, the detailed renderings of A. G. Smith show the development of American domestic architecture step by step. The arrangement is primarily chronological: the Indians, the Northern Colonial tradition, the Southern Colonial tradition, and the various styles that found widespread favor after the establishment of the Republic.

The building on page 34 is maintained by the Preservation Society of Newport County, Newport, R.I.

Published in Canada by General Publishing Company, Ltd., 30 Lesmill Road, Don Mills, Toronto, Ontario.

The American House Styles of Architecture Coloring Book is a new work, first published by Dover Publications, Inc., in 1983.

International Standard Book Number: 0-486-24472-5

Manufactured in the United States of America
Dover Publications, Inc., 180 Varick Street, New York, N.Y. 10014

Taos Pueblo (*N.M.*, *pre-sixteenth century*). The oldest permanent habitations in this country are perhaps the large communal dwellings of the Pueblo Indians of the Southwest. These structures were built of sundried adobe bricks with mud used as mortar. The units were built one on top of the other with one family's roof being the terrace of the next. The roofs were supported by logs laid closely across the tops of the wall and covered with brush and adobe. The thick walls required by this method of construction provided excellent insulation in the hot, dry climate. When the Spanish colonists arrived in the Southwest they had the local Pueblo tribes build their missions, churches and administration buildings. The architecture of the region has retained much of its original character to this day.

Saltbox House (*Jethro Coffin House, Nantucket, Mass., ca. 1686*). The first English colonists in New England built one-room rectangular houses with a stone chimney on one end. The easiest way to add another room to an existing house was by the addition of a lean-to across the back. The house then took on the shape of a saltbox. The Jethro Coffin House dem- onstrates a further refinement: with the addition of a parlor the large chimney became central and the salt- box reached its fullest development. The central chimney was an important feature in a cold climate, as the surrounding rooms insulated it from heat loss to the exterior.

Jettied House (*Parson Capen House, Topsfield, Mass., 1683*). The origins of this style of gabled farmhouse can be traced to the Middle Ages. Such framed houses were common in southeast England during the Elizabethan era. Characteristic of this heritage is the jettied second story with its framed overhang and pendills or corner drops. Other typical elements are the massive central chimney and the casement windows. The substantial and secure residence of Parson Joseph Capen indicates the prominent position of the minister in the New England Puritan communities. Jettied houses are often confused with garrison houses, but the true garrison house, more in the nature of a fort, was found only on the frontier.

Cape Cod Cottage (*Bass River Farm, Cape Cod, Mass.*). The Cape Cod house was a development of the late seventeenth or early eighteenth century. It grew from a simple cottage of one bay to a "full-sized" house of two bays around a central chimney. The example illustrated here has a bowed or rainbow roof, an innovation developed by local ships' carpenters. It added a little extra headroom to the second floor. The Cape Cod house is typically covered with weathered gray shingles and has outside shutters.

Hudson Valley Dutch (*Bries House, East Greenbush, N.Y., 1723*). Brick was the favorite building material of the early Dutch settlers in the Hudson Valley. The earliest Dutch houses had steep roofs with stepped gables, but by 1700 the gables were straight with one step or elbow at the lower corners. Perhaps the chief distinguishing feature of these houses is the setting of the roof inside the gable. The bricks in these gables were often set in elaborate patterns. Cross-shaped anchor irons were used to fasten the timbers supporting the roof and floors to the masonry wall.

Flemish Farmhouse (*Dyckman House, N.Y., N.Y., 1783*). This house was originally a small bakehouse with a massive stone chimney. As its owner prospered, the house proper was built, incorporating the features of the locally prevailing Flemish tradition, including a gambrel roof with flaring eaves. In later versions these were extended to form a veranda. In the typical early Dutch gambrel, the break in the gable is near the ridge of the roof. Additions to existing houses, made by adding wings to either or both sides, provided space for married children or grandparents.

Log Cabin (*a surviving example from the southern Appalachian Mountains, N.C.*). For thousands of years the construction of shelters from logs had been a natural response to the heavily wooded environment of Northern Europe. The peasants opening new land in the forests of Germany and Scandinavia had developed many variations of layout and techniques of construction. When Northern European settlers came to the American frontier, they brought these methods with them. At first, temporary shelters were built of rough logs left round and only notched at the corners. The chimneys of these cabins were of sticks and clay. In time, permanent houses were built of logs hewn square, dovetailed and chinked with clay. Carefully built stone chimneys were another sign of permanence. Porches might also be added. Some of these houses have survived for more than two hundred years.

Virginia Farmhouse (*Adam Thoroughgood House, Princess Anne County, Va., ca. 1636–40*). Although the earliest farmhouses in Virginia were of wood, the English planters soon aspired to build themselves brick "manor houses" as means permitted. This house, with its steep roof and pyramidal chimney, came out of an English Tudor tradition. The diamond-shaped windowpanes give the house a medieval effect. The brick of the Thoroughgood house is laid in the traditional manner known as English bond.

Maryland T-Plan House (*Otwell House, Md., 1670*). Built by a planter of considerable means, this house consists of two rectangular structures joined to form a T. The main structure contains a hall and parlor; the back wing, the dining room and kitchen. Chimneys were placed at the end of each wing. The main advantage of the T-plan was that it provided cross ventilation in a warm climate. The gambrel roof provided ample space for the bedrooms on the second floor, which received light and ventilation through windows in the "watershed" dormers.

Early Georgian Town House (*Letitia Street House, Philadelphia, Pa., 1714*). This town house was developed from an earlier Colonial type—the Swedish three-room plan, which was recommended by William Penn to the early settlers. The brick is laid in a pattern known as Flemish bond. The large chimney located to one side served corner fireplaces in the two rooms in the main floor. The cove molding under the eaves, the large sash windows and the paneled shutters are all early Georgian features. The scrolled supports of the door hood are a Wren Baroque element (town houses much like this, designed by Sir Christopher Wren, were common in London at the time).

Georgian Transitional (*Cupola House, Edenton, N.C., ca. 1725*). The coastal region of North Carolina was a melting pot of Colonial architectural styles. This house combines features from several locations and periods. The jettied second floor, supported by brackets, and the steep roof are a New England influence. The sloped chimney offsets and the oval window in the front gable can be traced to Virginia. The later Georgian cupola and sash windows were added when the house was remodeled in 1758.

German Stone House (*Hager's Fancy, Hagerstown, Md., 1740*). The early German settlers of Pennsylvania and western Maryland found stone readily available for the construction of houses much like those they remembered from Bavaria or Moravia. The American versions retained much of their medieval flavor. They had narrow pent roofs, protecting the doors and windows of the lower floor from the elements, running along the house partially or entirely. In the Hager house, the pent roof has been widened to become a porch. In typically German fashion, the house was built into a hillside over a spring. The cool cellar was used for the storage of milk, butter and other dairy products.

Philadelphia Georgian (*Mount Pleasant, Philadelphia, Pa., 1762*). The most elaborate houses in the Colonies were built in Philadelphia. Most were of masonry construction and quite ambitious in scale. Mount Pleasant was built of stone rubble covered with stucco to resemble finished stone. The corner quoins and the stringcourse are of brick. The tin-covered hip roof is topped by a balustrade. Typically Georgian details include a Palladian window in the center of the pedimented pavilion and Doric pilasters flanking the doorway. Above the door is a fine fanlight. This impressive house was built by a wealthy sea captain, John MacPherson.

New England Georgian (*Richard Derby House, Salem, Mass., 1762*). The Derby House is of brick construction with a gambrel roof. The facade of this and other Georgian houses was perfectly symmetrical. The large double chimneys on each end of the house further contribute to the feeling of stability and balance. Of special interest in this example are the arched windows and the fluted pilasters supporting the pediment over the door.

Louisiana Plantation House (*Homeplace Plantation, St. Charles Parish, La., ca. 1801*). The Homeplace Plantation is an example of the French raised-cottage tradition at its fullest development. The style evolved as a response to the hot, humid environment of the bayou country. The main living area, raised above its often muddy surroundings, was able to catch any breeze that might be stirring. Construction was based on traditional French methods, combining stuccoed brick with plastered vertical timbers on the upper level. The wide porches or galleries provided access and ventilation to each room through French doors.

Adam (*Cook-Oliver House, Salem, Mass., 1802*). The Adam Style, dominant during the Federal Period, was named after its English developer, the architect Robert Adam. Its principles were based on the study of Greek archeology. The delicacy of detail, including the slender columns, gives the style a feeling of light-ness and elegance. In New England one of the main advocates of the Adam Style was Samuel McIntire, a woodcarver and architect from Salem. The Cook-Oliver House was one of a series he built there. Mc-Intire was especially known for the fineness of wood ornament on his houses.

Adam Town House (*Gadsen House, Charleston, S.C., ca. 1800*). This tall, narrow town house is typical of those built in Charleston during the Federal Period. Many Southern planters maintained town houses for entertaining during the social season in addition to their plantation houses in the country.

The main reception rooms in the town houses were located on the high second floor with large windows that opened onto a broad porch overlooking the garden. The elevated location of the rooms helped them catch cool breezes blowing in from the bay.

Greek Revival (*Belle Grove Plantation, White Castle, La., 1857*). Greek Revival architecture began to be popular in America around 1820. This revival was not just a "surface style," as were many that were to follow it, but actually had a basis in form. Its advocates, believing the Greek temple to be the perfect model of proportion, style and ornament, designed public buildings and private houses accordingly. The Greek Revival mansion reached the height of its development on the prosperous plantations of Louisiana and Mississippi in the decades just before the Civil War. Belle Grove, with its fluted columns topped by Corinthian capitals, is an excellent example.

Half-Timbered House (*Moravian cottage, Mo., 1850*). Moravian pioneers from Pennsylvania and new immigrants to the American frontier from Germany held fast to their building traditions. Although it looks as if it belonged in the Black Forest in medieval days, this house was actually built on Missouri territory in the mid-nineteenth century. The half-timbered construction technique involved pegging together the timbers on the ground, erecting and assembling them vertically and filling the spaces between them with bricks that were plastered over and whitewashed.

Jeffersonian Classicism (*Monticello, Albemarle County, Va., 1770–1809*). Thomas Jefferson designed and built his home, Monticello, over a period of almost forty years, during which it underwent many changes. The early fathers of the American Republic identified themselves with the founders of Republican Rome in spirit and taste. Jefferson sought to give visible form to the new concepts of freedom and democracy. When he was asked to design the Virginia state capitol in 1784, he rejected the Georgian and Regency styles, which were then popular for public buildings in England, and chose instead to base his design on Roman

buildings he had seen in France. In designing Monticello, Jefferson also used elements he had seen in
French Neoclassic buildings, including the portico
with its Roman pediment and rotunda topped by the
Palladian dome. Balustraded promenades extend
from the house on each side. Covered passages leading to the kitchen, stables and servants' quarters ran
beneath them. Other innovations included a dumb-
waiter and an indoor toilet—considered advanced for
its time. The construction was of brick with white
wood trim.

Carpenter's Gothic (*Delamater House, Rhinebeck, N.Y., 1844*). Although their medieval European models were built of stone, many of the early Gothic Revival houses in America were built of wood—hence the term Carpenter's Gothic. The distinguishing features of the Gothic style are pointed window arches, high pitched gables topped with pinnacles, and an elaboration of tracery. Early Gothic Revival houses were painted in subtle variations of gray and brown. The Delamater House was designed by one of the style's leading architects, Alexander Jackson Davis.

Italian Villa (*Morse-Libby House, Portland, Me., 1859–63*). Although originally based on the design of Italian farmhouses, the American Italianate villa could be quite grand. The facade was asymmetrical, usually with a tower to one side. Wall surfaces were of smooth stone or stuccoed brick with rustication, if any, in the form of corner quoins. Roofs either had low gables or were hipped. The Morse-Libby House has both types of roof. The windows were typically arched and often hooded.

Octagon House (*Farmington, Me., ca. 1850–60*). The Octagon Style was a variation of the Victorian Italianate, promoted by an eccentric phrenologist, Orson Squire Fowler, during the 1850s and 1860s. The rooms on each floor were arranged around a central hall and stairway. The cupola on the low-pitched roof provided both ventilation and light to the interior hall. This example is built of brick with a poured-concrete foundation. Fowler advocated poured-concrete slabs for construction—an innovation in his day.

Moorish Revival (*Longwood, Natchez, Miss., 1860*). The Victorian craze for revival architecture left few historic sources untouched. This elaborate fantasy, with its Moorish dome, windows and detail, was de-signed by Samuel Sloan as the residence of Haller Nutt. The house, begun in 1860 but left unfinished, became known as Nutt's Folly.

High-Victorian Gothic (*Earlville, N.Y., ca. 1875*). This style combines all the elements of the earlier Gothic styles at once—the pointed Gothic windows, the Italianate tower, stickwork in the gable and a liberal application of frilly ironwork. The single most characteristic feature of the High-Victorian Gothic Style was elaborate coloration, achieved through the use of varied materials on single surfaces and by painting the walls and trim with highly contrasting colors and tones. This approach differs greatly from the muted coloration of the early Gothic Revival houses.

Second Empire (*cottage, Bangor, Me., ca. 1870*). The style was very popular in France in the mid-nineteenth century and its influence was soon felt across the Atlantic. In this cottage we see it in almost pure form. Its two pavilions, mansard roof with dormered windows, Ionic columns and iron window grilles are all characteristic features. Decorative cast-iron fences were also fashionable during this period.

Stick Style (*Emlen Physick House, Cape May, N.J., 1879*). Although this style finds its historical precedent in the Elizabethan half-timbered house, it is typically Victorian in its massiveness. Stickwork patterning was applied to the exterior wall surfaces to create a half-timbered effect. The vertical stickwork, combined with steep roofs, emphasized tall proportions. Extensive porches, supported by posts with diagonal bracing, give a further Victorian feeling of "character."

Queen Anne (*Los Angeles Historical Society, Los Angeles, Calif., ca. 1890*). The Queen Anne Style, the first of the "surface styles," was popular in America from the late 1870s through the 1890s. Variety of form, color, texture and materials distinguishes the style. A single house may combine stone, shingles, brick and half-timbering, with accents of Gothic, Renaissance and Romanesque detail. All this may be topped off with a massive chimney paneled in molded brick. Bay windows and gabled porches were frequently used, as were turrets during the latter stages of the style's development. Windows could be either round or flat-topped, and stained glass was often used in stairwells and in transoms above windows and doors.

Shingle (*Isaac Bell House, Newport, R.I., 1882–83*). The Shingle Style superseded the Queen Anne Style as the height of fashion in the 1880s. Although it has some features in common with the Queen Anne (turrets, windows, chimneys) it is much simpler. The ground floor was sometimes of masonry construction; the rest of the house was covered entirely by shingles. This house was designed by Stanford White of the famous architectural firm McKim, Mead & White.

Richardson Romanesque (*Ayer House, Chicago, Ill., ca. 1882*). H. H. Richardson introduced the Romanesque Revival Style. As it was adopted by other architects (as in this house, by Burnham and Root) it became known as Richardson Romanesque. It is iden-tified by massive conical towers, rough stone surfaces, and windows and arcades, often deeply recessed, with rounded arches. Buildings in this style have a fortress-like sense of strength.

Chateauesque (*Augustus Byram Residence, Chicago, Ill., 1882*). This grand style was brought to America from France in the late 1860s, but did not develop fully until the 1880s. It is based on the Italian Renaissance and French Gothic traditions brought together during the reign of François I in the early sixteenth century. Its revival in France occurred in the second quarter of the nineteenth century. Characteristic of the Chateauesque Style are an asymmetrical facade, steep hipped roofs, elaborate chimneys and gables with pinnacles. The windows are deep-set and have thick masonry mullions. Such houses were always built of stone or brick.

Sod House (*Okla.*, 1894). When homesteaders settled on the Great Plains they found very few trees for lumber. They therefore turned to the only material available—the prairie sod itself—to construct houses. Special plows were used to cut strips of sod three or four inches thick and twelve to fourteen inches wide.

These blocks were then laid up much as brick would be. Windows were framed with wood. The roof was made of planks covered with sod. These houses were well insulated, being cool in summer and warm in winter.

Beaux-Arts Classical (*Hermann Oelrichs Residence, Newport, R.I., 1902*). The Oelrichs mansion is another Newport creation of Stanford White, but in a much more pretentious style than the Bell House (p. 30). The Beaux-Arts Style, brought to America by architects who had studied at the École des Beaux-Arts in Paris, attempted to combine elements of both Greek and Roman Classicism. Its most easily recognized characteristic is its use of grouped columns and arches. The style was used for many libraries, courthouses and other public buildings.

Art Nouveau (*Albert Sullivan House, Chicago, Ill., 1892*). This modest row house was built by Louis Sullivan, one of the country's most famous early modern architects, for his brother. Although the door, with its rounded arch, and the columns in the window recess are Romanesque-influenced, the simplicity of form is pure Sullivan. The geometric interlacing ornament is in the Art Nouveau tradition. Much of Sullivan's best-known work was done in the Midwest.

Prairie (*Frederick C. Robie House, Chicago, Ill., 1908*). This house, designed by Frank Lloyd Wright, is an advanced example of the Prairie Style. Wright advocated an "organic architecture" in which the house should be in complete harmony with its envi-ronment. The long lines of the Prairie house are intended to parallel the flatness of the Midwestern landscape. The large central chimney is also a feature of the style, the fireplace being an important element of many Wright interiors.

Bungalow (*Los Angeles, Calif., 1910*). The bungalow, a type of small one-story house developed in California by the Greene Brothers, is marked by its low roof and verandas. The example shown here is in the Western Stick Style. Since the bungalow was economical, the style became very popular. It spread quickly across the country, spawning many regional variations.

Prairie-Style Bungalow (*T. S. Estabrook House, Oak Park, Ill., 1908*). Although much of Wright's work was on larger commissions, here he has applied the principles of the Prairie Style to a modest bungalow. It has the central chimney, low-pitched roof and wings that give it the interior spaciousness characteristic of the style. The comfort of Wright's houses was widely recognized and appreciated, and his influence soon spread throughout America and Europe.

Pueblo (*Zimmerman House, Albuquerque, N.M., 1929*). The Pueblo Style is a regional revival style. It began in California at the turn of the century and soon spread throughout the Southwest. Based upon the dwellings of the Pueblo Indians, this style incorporates the organic qualities and massiveness of the original dwellings, adapting them to contemporary needs and lifestyles. The Pueblo Style house is built of adobe or of masonry that is plastered to give it the appearance of adobe. Roof timbers extend through the walls, and corners are often irregularly rounded. The style is still in use in the Southwest today.

Spanish Colonial Revival (*Cravens House, Oklahoma City, Okla., 1929*). The buildings of the early Spanish settlers in the Southwest were the inspiration for this revival. Low-pitched roofs covered with red tile are a hallmark of the Spanish Colonial house. The masonry walls are stuccoed, and balconies with iron railings are frequently used. Doors are often recessed in arcades. The style was not limited to the Southwest but spread across the entire country. It was especially popular in Florida. To this style we owe the patio, so popular in today's suburban lifestyle.

International (*Marcel Breuer House, Lincoln, Mass., 1939*). Houses in the International Style were designed from the inside out, the function of the interior spaces determining exterior form and appearance. This idea, originated by Frank Lloyd Wright, was soon incorporated into the principles of the Bauhaus School in Germany and further developed. At the outbreak of World War II, many prominent European architects emigrated to the United States. Walter Gropius, Marcel Breuer and Mies van der Rohe brought the new International Style with them.

Miesian (*Philip Johnson Residence, New Canaan, Conn., 1948*). Known as the Glass House, the building was designed by the architect Philip Johnson as his own residence. It is an excellent example of the Miesian Style, developed by Ludwig Mies van der Rohe, of which Johnson was an advocate. It is based on the principles of skeletal construction, in which an exterior frame, rather than the walls themselves, supports the structure. Not having to bear weight, the walls may be made of any material—in this case, glass. Many modern office towers are designed on these principles.

Contemporary House (*designed by John Milnes Baker, 1981*). In the 1970s architects became more concerned with efficiency of construction and economy of operation in the design of houses. Houses built today must be well insulated, with double-glazed windows. Many houses are designed to be solar-heated.

Open interior space and accommodation for informal lifestyles are popular today. Decks and patios are used for entertaining. The house's redwood siding is typical of the trend back to the use of natural materials in home building.

DOVER COLORING BOOKS

FAVORITE ROSES COLORING BOOK, Ilil Arbel. (25845-9) $2.95

FUN WITH SEARCH-A-WORD COLORING BOOK, Nina Barbaresi. (26327-4) $2.50

FUN WITH SPELLING COLORING BOOK, Nina Barbaresi. (25999-4) $2.50

JEWISH HOLIDAYS AND TRADITIONS COLORING BOOK, Chaya Burstein. (26322-3) $2.95

INDIAN TRIBES OF NORTH AMERICA COLORING BOOK, Peter F. Copeland. (26303-7) $2.95

BIRDS OF PREY COLORING BOOK, John Green. (25989-7) $2.95

LIFE IN ANCIENT EGYPT COLORING BOOK, John Green and Stanley Appelbaum. (26130-1) $2.95

WHALES AND DOLPHINS COLORING BOOK, John Green. (26306-1) $2.95

DINOSAUR ABC COLORING BOOK, Llyn Hunter. (25786-X) $2.50

SHARKS OF THE WORLD COLORING BOOK, Llyn Hunter. (26137-9) $2.95

HISTORY OF SPACE EXPLORATION COLORING BOOK, Bruce LaFontaine. (26152-2) $2.95

HOLIDAYS STAINED GLASS COLORING BOOK, Ted Menten. (26062-3) $3.95

FUN WITH OPPOSITES COLORING BOOK, Anna Pomaska and Suzanne Ross. (25983-8) $2.50

DINOSAUR LIFE ACTIVITY BOOK, Donald Silver and Patricia Wynne. (25809-2) $2.50

HISTORY OF THE AMERICAN AUTOMOBILE COLORING BOOK, A. G. Smith and Randy Mason. (26315-0) $2.95

THE VELVETEEN RABBIT COLORING BOOK, Margery Williams and Thea Kliros. (25924-2) $2.95

HEBREW ALPHABET COLORING BOOK, Chaya Burstein. (25089-X) $2.95

COLUMBUS DISCOVERS AMERICA COLORING BOOK, Peter F. Copeland. (25542-5) $2.75

STORY OF THE AMERICAN REVOLUTION COLORING BOOK, Peter Copeland. (25648-0) $2.95

FAVORITE POEMS FOR CHILDREN COLORING BOOK, illustrated by Susan Gaber. (23923-3) $2.95

HORSES OF THE WORLD COLORING BOOK, John Green. (24985-9) $2.95

WILD ANIMALS COLORING BOOK, John Green. (25476-3) $2.95

THE DAYS OF THE DINOSAUR COLORING BOOK, MATTHEW KALMENOFF. (25359-7) $2.95

SMALL ANIMALS OF NORTH AMERICA COLORING BOOK, Elizabeth A. McClelland. (24217-X) $2.95

Paperbound unless otherwise indicated. Prices subject to change without notice. Available at your book dealer or write for free catalogues to Dept. 23, Dover Publications, Inc., 31 East 2nd Street, Mineola, N.Y. 11501. Please indicate field of interest. Each year Dover publishes over 200 books on fine art, music, crafts and needlework, antiques, languages, literature, children's books, chess, cookery, nature, anthropology, science, mathematics, and other areas.

Manufactured in the U.S.A.